"GORDY-ISMS"

Engineer castle

Also by Gordon L. Ewell

DUNG IN MY FOXHOLE

A SOLDIER'S ACCOUNT OF THE IRAQ WAR AND HIS POSTWAR STRUGGLES WITH INJURY AND PTSD THROUGH POETRY

A LIFETIME AT WAR

LIFE AFTER BEING SEVERELY WOUNDED IN COMBAT—NEVER ENDING DUNG

"GORDY-ISMS"

Inspiring, Inspirational and Thought-Provoking Quotes from the Mind of a Severely Wounded Combat Veteran; Proverbial Dung

GORDON L EWELL

Order this book online at www.trafford.com
or email orders@trafford.com

Most Trafford titles are also available at major online book retailers.

Printed in the United States of America.

ISBN: 978-1-4669-6712-0 (sc)
ISBN: 978-1-4669-6711-3 (hc)
ISBN: 978-1-4669-6710-6 (e)

Library of Congress Control Number: 2012920921

Trafford rev. 11/12/2012

www.trafford.com

North America & international
toll-free: 1 888 232 4444 (USA & Canada)
phone: 250 383 6864 • fax: 812 355 4082

For Scarlett Olivia and Lincoln Abbygale,
Daddy's Princesses

People will forget what you said. People will forget what you did. But people will never forget how you made them feel.

—Maya Angelou

Contents

LIST OF ILLUSTRATIONS

Illustrations are listed in the order which they appear. First is its name, then it's location within the book

PREFACE

If only I could hold the moment—to reach out my hand and stop time. But in this I err. For to hold the note is to spoil the song.

—Richard Paul Evans

If I had but a quarter for every time I wished that I could stop time, or rather go back in time and then stop time, I would be a millionaire. I was severely injured in the war in Iraq in 2006. A career soldier, I was proud of my chosen profession. I was honored to be a defender of freedom. I was among the very best at what I did as a soldier. When I was called upon to go to war, of course I had some fears. But one thing I knew is that I would come home. I had confidence in my skills, my training, and knew well the dangers of my mission and was prepared for it. I knew I would be successful and come home. I never dreamed I would come home severely wounded. My mission was, in a nutshell, to find the roadside bombs and ensure other teams with this dangerous mission had the latest intelligence, the skills, and the equipment to be successful as well. At the time, there were over three thousand one hundred roadside bombs being found or finding our soldiers every month, over one hundred every day. A vehicle I was riding in was blown up on six different occasions. One bomb blast too many left me severely wounded . . . permanently disabled for the rest of my life. Something I never dreamed would happen. With a long, lonely, and painful recovery road to travel—to get put back together as best that forty-nine different health care specialists, surgeries, stays in six different hospitals in three different states, including a level one polytrauma hospital in Palo Alto, California, and years of therapies afterward could do—I found myself many times wanting to stop time prior to getting wounded in combat. I didn't want to have a broken neck, a severe traumatic brain injury, and permanent neurological damage. I did not want to lose an eye, to be legally blind and deaf. I didn't want to need a wheelchair, a walker, and canes to get around. I didn't want to never be able to drive a vehicle again, to be homebound, to be in chronic pain, or to suffer daily with post-traumatic stress syndrome (PTSD). I didn't want to be on a liquid diet for over four years while getting my face and mouth rebuilt. I wanted to stop time to a period in my past when I was happy, carefree, and in prime physical condition. But indeed, six years now have passed, and I realize now, as author Richard Paul Evans said, "To hold the note is to spoil the song!" Though broken, I have been blessed beyond measure, in ways I could never could have been, or even imagined, prior to my combat injuries. To "hold the note," I would have missed a very beautiful song. I have an appreciation for and depth of understanding for life and love and the fragility of both I never would have ever had. I have an appreciation and an eye for the beauty in everything around me I never would have seen before. I am grateful for my life. I feel blessed.

Just what is a Gordy-ism?

There were times during my recovery and rehabilitation, years in fact, that were very dark and full of pain and agony. More than once, suicide seemed like a brighter alternative. Just to make it through a single day was a big victory. I told myself, if I could think of just one single positive thought, or a thing to be thankful for at the beginning of each day, that when pain or dark images were getting unbearable, if I could pull out my thought and read it out loud or even just hold the small piece of paper I wrote it on in a closed fist, it would help me get through the darkness. Or at least let enough light in that I could just make it through the day. I would focus on one day at a time, just a day at a time. I would do this every day. It seemed to help. I soon began sharing my daily thoughts with others who were fighting their own battles of recovery, along with me, in different hospital stays, and with a few people in general that were close to me. They began to look forward to my little daily thoughts to share with them.

My first name is Gordon. Everyone calls me Gordy.

My peers began to refer to my thoughts for the day as Gordy-isms.

It stuck, and so began the birth of Gordy-isms, and it is a practice I continue to do each day. I think of something positive each morning and write it down to start my day. I now share them in my writings and on the computer with others via the Internet on my websites and Facebook pages.

So what are Gordy-isms?

They are short and inspirational, uplifting, or thought-provoking little quip-its, or intended to be anyway. A little thought to start your day with a smile.

I hope you enjoy them! I hope they bring smiles, warm your heart when needed, and perhaps provide a laugh or two when needed as well.

I don't profess to be full of profound wisdom or have some superior depth of intellectual insight into the mind, body, and soul or profess to have the answers to any questions.

I am just a broken ol' warrior who tries to get a couple of brain cells to bump into each other in the morning and spark a little thought to start my day off on a good note. I am my own little blue-collar philosopher, if you will.

Thank you for letting me share with you my Gordy-isms!

SECTION ONE

Friends and Friendship

Coffee hands

Good friends are like a warm cup of coffee nestled gently between your hands, on a chilly, brisk morning.

Dear friends come in all shapes, sizes, colors, races, creeds, and classes. However, they *all* have *one* thing in common. They *all* love you! Don't be the exception. Return the *love*!

When crossing fast-moving streams that often run through the path of life we are traveling, good friends are like the solid stepping stones that will hold you up and allow you to cross the stream without getting your feet wet!

When your world seems to be weighing heaviest upon your shoulders, a dear friend can always find a way to fill your world with helium.

A good visit with old friends is a good reminder of what is truly important in life. It is not titles or what you own. It is love and how you choose to share it with others.

No matter how much real time passes between visits with a true friend, when reunited, you can pick up conversations and talk as if you had just seen each other the day before. What a wonderful thing!

Coffee is so good in part to its hidden meaning. *Coffee* stands for *c*ome *o*ver *f*or *f*riendship *e*veryone *e*njoys!

Dear and true friends seem to have the ability to not be bound by the rules of Father Time or the laws of physics. I do not know how else to explain why they are *always*, with perfect timing, there when you need someone to laugh with, a shoulder to cry on, someone to listen to you, or someone just to give you a pat on the back, a handshake, or a hug.

If they are not close enough to speak directly to, dear friends are never more than about a foot away in two directions—either up to wonderful memories in your mind, or down to precious memories in your heart!

It is not often that a person finds a true friend—someone who wants nothing more than an ear to listen, a shoulder for a tear to land on, a laugh at a good joke, even a laugh at a bad joke, and the knowledge that they would do anything for you, most often before you ever had to ask.

One of the best gifts for any occasion cannot be bought. It is found with humility in the heart, contained within a big hug, presented with the sincere smile of dear friendship, and given verbally by simply looking happily into the eyes of the receiver and saying "I love you!"

While cruising down the highway of life, good friends are the suspension on our vehicle. They help absorb the shock of the bumps, potholes, and rocks in the road which could cause pain and misery and help make the ride of life as smooth and enjoyable as possible!

It is a fact that laughter is good medicine, social interaction keeps the mind active, and getting rid of stress can ward off a heart attack. These things are provided by a dear friend. And it is easy to have many—simply be one for someone else! Just think of the many health problems you could avoid and help someone else avoid by simply being kind, being a good listener, sharing laughs, and being willing to open your heart.

The kindness of friends reminds me that there is a reason I sit on my wallet and not my heart. It is much more important that my heart has room to swell with happiness than my wallet having room to buy things that will never last as long as a precious moment with a friend.

You know you have found a dear and special friend when they will resort to trying to simulate grotesque sounds of unpleasant bodily functions, or hang spaghetti out of their nose in an attempt to cheer you up and get you to laugh when you are feeling blue.

There is no void a true friend cannot fill. They laugh with you, laugh at you, lift you up when you are down, knock you down if you are too full of yourself (hee-hee), and are there to congratulate, console, counsel, listen, love, worry, and cry with you, whether tears of joy or sorrow. They are few and far between, so when one enters your life, make sure that you keep them there, by being all they are for you, for them!

No matter where you or your dear friends are in the world, they are always as close as your heart. With today's technology and a few finger strokes, they can also be as close as your ears and the sound of their voice can be a like beautiful song in your head within seconds. Don't let distance, distance a friendship. Give them a call today.

Good friends are like a warm cup of coffee nestled gently between your hands, on a chilly, brisk morning.

We have ambition and strong willpower to enable us to chase all that we can dream of and choose. When it appears, as if we are going to come up short, there always seems to be that special friend who just happens to show up at just the right time to motivate us to keep chasing and never lose sight of our dreams.

The wealth of my heart, happiness, self-worth—however you phrase it, you feel at your very best not by looking in your wallet, in your purse, or at your bank statement but rather by leading with your heart, taking risks, and doing your best to be the best friend you can be. Often it is a close friend who is the recipient of your best works. It could also be the good fortune, if you choose it, to let the recipient be a total stranger.

Friendships are not maintenance free. Even the best of friendships require some effort to let friends know you love and care about them. They cannot thrive if you always take and never give back.

What makes a person special, important, respected, admired, and adored is *not* the medals he wears upon his chest, certificates on a wall in his home or office, or worldly titles that precede or follow his name. No, what makes a person special is nothing on the outside. It is *everything* from within him—a big heart full of charity and love; kindness; compassion; good thoughts; ability to think of others; a desire to help, aid, assist, and provide; being quick to laugh, compliment, and listen; and being slow to belittle and judge—all of which are manifested through actions on the outside that tend to draw others to you and you to others and lay a firm foundation for friendships, love, admiration, and respect to be built upon!

Kindness is so special it was designed to be able to be delivered in many different packages: a warm smile, a gentle touch, a friendly wink of an eye, a kind word, a softly spoken voice, the wave of a hand, a kiss . . . No matter how you package and deliver it, friendly kindness will always be well received.

Just when you think you have found a mountain too high to climb, good friends have a way of letting you know that God gave them extra carabiners, pitons, and rope for you to climb it with.

Winged heart in healing

Life is tough Pilgrim. It's even tougher if you're stupid!

—John Wayne

SECTION TWO

Lighthearted

Glass half-full

It doesn't matter if you see the glass as half-empty or half-full. If you are thirsty, be smart enough to drink it! Either way, it will quench your thirst, and that should give you something to smile about.

Be a believer! Believe in faith, fairies, miracles, angels, dreams, and pixie dust! It will make you smile; and who knows? It just may be angels, fairies, or pixie dust working on you. Believe!

Tears are the Miracle-Gro that nourishes flowers of the heart.

If you are dead set on judging a book by its cover, make sure it's *your* story that is written on the inside flap.

If your heart is in the right place, you may not be able to hear it beat, but someone else will—loud and clear!

Jump in your car, and no matter how fast you drive, there are three things you can never outrun: your past, a lie, and the police radio telling the patrol car up ahead how fast you were clocked driving through the speed trap.

The reason pets can't talk is because God did not want us to feel constantly embarrassed by how much more common sense they have than we do.

We all have two of the following: eyes, ears, nostrils, arms, hands, legs, and feet. So why only one mouth? Because to make someone's day, takes *one* little smile!

If you like yourself and feel good inside and out and have peace of mind, you are beautiful! If you can do the things you want without easily tiring, you are healthy! If both of these apply, I don't care what your bathroom scale says. You are beautiful and healthy! When I become dictator, I will outlaw bathroom scales.

If you don't believe grown men cry, just walk into any bar or club at closing time on a Saturday night and look around when you hear the bartender holler out, "Last call!" You could irrigate five acres of farm land with all the big ol' alligator tears you'll see well up in eyes of every grown man in the place.

Laughter is good medicine. But with all medicines, there are side effects. You may experience sore cheeks from oversized smiles, sore ribs from continuous laughing, or even a rare bladder discharge from uncontrollable laughter. In spite of the side effects, it is one medicine I wish everyone could be prescribed, could share, and even have an occasional overdose of.

Laugh when you're happy. Cry if you're blue. Bite your tongue if you're angry. To blow your cool only makes you a fool!

Plan for the worst, hope and pray for the best, and count your blessings if things fall somewhere in between.

Someday we will all meet our Maker; will you be labeled a giver or taker? Will you be able to look him square in the eye, be given wings, and to heaven take flight? Or will you be ashamed, stare down at your feet, and hear the words "Just keep walking that way, best of luck, it's quite steep."

Doing math this morning, I realized that when we help others, we *subtract* from our own problems, we *add* to our feelings of happiness, our individual worries appear to get *divided* in half, while our blessings are instantly *multiplied*.

Kind words and actions both have the same roots: kind thoughts!

If you can't smile through some of life's little problems, at least stand on your head through them. That way, your frown will look like a smile to others and not ruin their day as well.

If at first you don't succeed, try, try, try again . . . and again and again to find someone else to do it for you! I am so just kidding!

It doesn't matter if you see the glass as half-empty or half-full. If you are thirsty, be smart enough to drink it! Either way, it will quench your thirst, and that should give you something to smile about.

A review of my portfolio to ensure high dividends revealed I had had a good exchange rate with nieces and nephews. Friendships were diversified and giving high returns. Family was conservative and protected in vested accounts. Indeed, all was providing a high yield of happiness, thanks to my broker, my Creator.

If I wanted to see how wealthy I was, I would not run right to the bank. All I need to do is check my Facebook page. Thank you, my dear Facebook friends, for all your kind birthday wishes, blessings, inspiration, and support! You not only made me feel like a million dollars, you also left no doubt in my mind that I am one of the wealthiest and blessed people on our spinning orb (earth)! I love you all!

When you least expect it, a smile from a stranger will catch you off guard and give you reason to smile and feel a warmth in your heart as well. Why? That is just the magic of random acts of kindness. So have some fun and catch someone off guard. Simply wear a smile while waiting in the checkout line. Have fun!

Today I am going to actually do the things about which I keep saying, "I'll remember to do that tomorrow." Important things that often get over looked, like calling an old friend just see how they are doing, calling my parents to say "I love you," playing a game with my kids, and thanking my Creator that I am able to do these things! *Tomorrow*, I will mow the lawn.

A man who takes the time to sit a spell and ponder in depth on proverbs to tell is doing good to think wisely, with his heart and soul as well. But to constantly sit and spout words, not lifting a muscle to put them in action, becomes just a fool with his mouth constantly yacking.

It is impossible to frown with a smile in your heart and impossible to smile with a negative attitude.

When life seems to be beating up on you, rather than screaming and yelling like an idiot who crapped his pants, try laughing at the thought of some idiot you dislike crapping their pants. You might be surprised at how much smaller some of your problems will seem when you add a little humor to them.

When in doubt, smile! Smiles are contagious. So the worst that can happen is that someone else will smile too simply because you are!

Today, while enjoying some flowers in my yard, I got stung by a bee. At first, I was as mad as a hornet. But then I had to chuckle as I thought to myself, *This is a lesson of sharing*. Obviously, I am not the only person (or creature) that likes to enjoy the flowers. Next time, I will check to see if someone else is enjoying them before I stick my nose in.

Do you know why God did not spell the word *family* like this: *famile?* It is because it would have put the letters *m* and *e* in the word. A family is not about any "me." It is about a unit, a team, all working together in harmony for the good of the whole. While individuals within the unit are of great importance, it is how they interact as a whole that matters most. So says me, with love.

A good friend will tell you if you have something "unusual" hanging out of your nose, without making too much fun of you, to keep you from being embarrassed in public.

For the perfect smoothie, blend carefully two to three family members (that you like), a half-dozen good friends, a couple of neighbors (if you get along), a nice backyard, some shade, warm temperatures with a very light breeze, perfectly marinated meat of your choice, one big barbeque grill, potluck brought by the friends and neighbors, ice-cold beverages, music, some storytelling (both fact and fiction), and a lot of laughter. Enjoy all you can until you pass out, someone calls the police, or whoever fell into the fire pit cannot wait until morning to go to the emergency room (ha-ha).

I was thinking about the word *handicap,* not really liking it much, until it struck me: I believe it is an acronym to describe *hand*y, *i*nsightful, *cap*able persons, which we handicapped people are! Now I like it!

Start the week out by putting your best foot forward. The worst that can happen is some jerk will criticize your taste in shoes. However, there is always that same person who would do that if you were standing still.

Fads come and go—some are fast, some are slow, and some are generational. But there are a few things that have been and never will go out of style. These are a laugh, a smile, a kind word or gesture, a compliment, honesty, lending a helping hand, hard work, the innocence and imagination of children, freedom, justice, good morals, and love! These things will forever be welcomed and always be in style!

Don't be saddled by your burdens. There is a little cowboy in all of us. Rather, saddle your burdens and ride them like a bucking horse in a rodeo; ride them to the eight second buzzer and collect your prize money!

My thoughts on walking: if at first you don't succeed, fall, fall, fall sixty times, get some stitches, have some coffee, and try again!

I was brushing my teeth and thought, *I wonder what I can do today?* Then I had another thought that made me smile. Two of my brain cells must have accidently ran into each other as the thought came back: *You live in America! You can do anything you set your mind to!*

Three ways to start the week out right: (1) Let the driver that should have merged sooner cut in front of you on your commute. (2) Offer to let someone get on the elevator at work before you do. (3) Tell the person who serves you, even at a drive-through window, "Thank you for all you do." I guarantee you will get a smile or a wave that will make you feel good all over.

Everyone will get "their day," a day your ship will come in. You'll find the bottle with the genie in it. You will get a chance to enrich your life. When that day comes, will you be ready to make a wish or make a choice with a seconds notice? When you pick, will you choose to enrich your wallet? Or will you choose to enrich your heart? I hope that your heart account breaks the bank as you start off your week.

No doubt about it, its inventor sure put up a stink and had to put up with a lot of crap from the neighbors, local media, and I'm sure, even total strangers. But the man had a dream and didn't let people get to him even when they tried to "pee-pee" all over it! I thank God for his attitude and courage, as I am sure grateful for my indoor toilet!

Sometimes it is a good thing that one's mouth runs before they take the time to engage their brain. The consequences of this action is usually a good teacher of humility.

People are a lot like roses. To fully embrace and appreciate a rose, it is inevitable that at some time a thorn will prick you. Thorns do not take away from the beauty of a rose. You just have to take in stride, that while enjoying roses, every now and then, you will get pricked.

I truly believe that knowledge is power and that the pen is mightier than the sword. To keep from getting dehydrated, I have to actively water my thinker. One thing I try is letting the dictionary flop open and picking one new word definition to learn and trying to use it on someone during the day. If occasionally I pick a word that could get my beak broken, I do allow myself to pick again.

I believe that dreams come true if you want them to bad enough. Sometimes obstacles, time, or distance will make your dream appear unreachable; your path may get changed and seem to be leading you away from your dream. Many will give up or settle for less. But as long as you keep your dream in sight and stay determined, I believe you will find that the path will turn back toward it, and with determination not abandoned, the obstacles will get smaller. Keep chasing your dreams, and I believe that they can and will come true.

Sometimes I think we dream to have clarity of thought that we could not have with all the extra clutter that is on our minds during the day.

"Life is like a box of chocolates" (Forrest Gump). So true! If we do nothing with them, they could all melt and become nothing more than a great, big messy, sticky, rotten glob of goop. If you want to really enjoy life's chocolates before they melt, run around and share the box of chocolate with your family and friends. Then you will really enjoy every single one!

If we put as much effort into the small details of our lives as we do into the larger ones that others notice at first glance, I believe we would be surprised at how much better we would feel and how much better our outlook and attitude would be each day. "Don't sweat the small stuff," I have read, but don't totally overlook it either. It does not just magically go away.

Everyone will step in something along the path of life. It is inevitable. How you prepare for it, conduct yourself, and give of yourself to help to others, could make the difference of what you step in being a little piece bubble gum on your shoe or a big ol' pile of dung!

Commitment. Honor. The days are long gone where a handshake and a person's word were more of an unbreakable bond than a signature on any piece of paper.

God bless the optimists among us who remind me I need to put a better foot forward as I think dearly about our fellow man.

I was upset as could be when my world came crashing down all around me, until I realized it pushed a Starbucks within driving distance of my motorized wheelchair!

No matter the situation you find yourself in, from the right angle, you can always see that the glass is indeed half-full!

Change—the changing of the weather, the changing of the seasons, the changing of the tides—life is about changes, all kinds of changes, but change nonetheless. Even man's most solid, immovable statues to commemorate something or someone are about change. While the statue itself may not change, its appearance certainly does once a pigeon poops on it! Change . . .

I am grateful for American patriots who are not afraid to rattle the chains and shake the cobwebs out of the dormant minds of those who are uneducated in reality, lacking in common sense, and basically driving down life's highway asleep at the wheel!

When you get right down to it, life is about people and your interactions with them. If you truly want to be rich, nurture your interactions with everyone.

It is true if you really set your mind to doing something, you can achieve it. However, unless you intend on including your heart and putting all your heart into that which you set your mind, you will never really be giving your all to achieve your dream. Dream big, engage your heart and mind, and catch a dream!

If you walk alongside someone, a true friend will have you feeling as though you are walking on air, with the security of a solid smooth sidewalk under your feet, and with pleasant conversation. Before you know it, miles will be behind you.

If not so enriching and complementing to your life, a walk with alongside another will feel as though you are treading through snow, uphill, with miles to go and nothing to say. And they'll probably hit you up for money they'll never pay back along the way.

Touch, taste, smell, sight, sound, and something referred by some as the sixth sense of subconscious, or supernatural awareness—of all our senses, I believe the one that often fails people the most is what I call our seventh sense: common sense!

The me I was a moon ago . . . the me I am tonight . . . the me that I desire to be, underneath the next moon's light . . . Learn from your past and apply it to your future. I'll strive to be a better man tomorrow than today, that I may rest easier each night.

Beauty is indeed in the eye of the beholder. But what makes things truly beautiful comes from the value your heart places on them. While a rare Picasso painting is beautiful and worth millions to many, I would not trade a stick figure crayon picture from my kids that says "I Love You" on it, for all the Picasso's in the world.

There is beauty all around us. When we look with our hearts, we find some of the most beautiful things in the world cost nothing, yet are priceless. A look at God's canvas reminds us of that every day, in a sunrise, a sunset, a flower, majestic mountains, the waves of the ocean tides, and smiles of children . . . priceless beauty everywhere when one looks with their heart.

Blind faith: Listen to your heart and strive for things you think are beyond your grasp. Just think, if someone did not stand on a shore, staring at the horizon with determination and say, "I know there is something beyond what I can see," we would all still believe the world was flat!

I wish kindness was a secret. Then everyone would pass it on to at least one other person.

I would rather be broken in the land of liberty than 100 percent healthy and able to *only* wander in the lands and waters of the *rest* of the entire planet!

Walt Disney had it right: "It's a small world after all." I have a mind. I can think and reason. I can read and write, imagine and dream. Therefore, there is no place I cannot travel to—in my mind anyway.

There is a difference between having a big ego and being self-confident. Egos have to be fed and have to come first. A self-confident soul uses talents to feed others and eats last. I hate big egos. They don't look good on anyone.

There really is good, somewhere, in everyone whose path in life crosses or runs alongside our own. Often all it takes to bring that goodness out of someone is a small gesture of kindness: a friendly smile, a softly spoken hello, or just easing up on the throttle to let that someone on the highway come in front of you, even if it is them that should have yielded the right of way.

Nothing brightens a room, a day, or a heart quite like the smiles of children.

Though a short-lived life, what a joy it would be to be a big soft, fluffy snowflake softly descending to earth; loving a majestic and magnificent view; enjoying a beautiful, pristine descent; and then fading away into the innocent, illuminating laughter of children playfully engaged in a game of catching snowflakes on their tongue; and being lucky enough to be caught on an outstretched tongue of hope and then carried away on the magical giggle of achievement and success of a proud, sparkle-eyed child!

There are truly few things as beautiful as a being able to see an entire sky on a clear night, from horizon to horizon, full of stars, and void of any lights from cities or towns. The sheer beauty is not only breathtaking but also a reminder of just how tiny the space we occupy in relation to the rest of the universe.

The great things about smiles are the following: They are all beautiful. They are one size fits all (from ear to ear). They never go out of style. You can wear one with anything (or nothing, ha-ha). They feel great. They are fun to see on others. And they are the one thing that is contagious that you never have to worry about getting a shot to prevent them from spreading.

"Bite me!" is definitely not offensive if heard from a cheesecake, if you are not counting calories. Otherwise, use it with extreme caution.

When the people find they can vote themselves money, that will herald the end of the republic.

—Benjamin Franklin

SECTION THREE

Time and Money

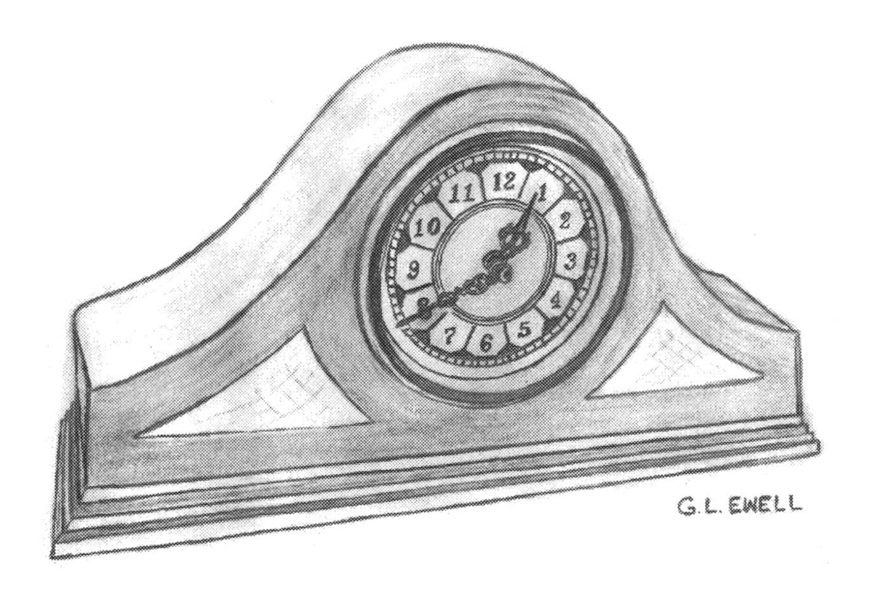

Mantle clock

Every single clock made has a magic feature to them that you cannot have removed or buy one without. No matter the make, model, or where it was made, the day will come that the feature activates, and you'll look at the clock and say, "Where in the hell did the time go?"

Time is one of our most precious commodities. Our time is valuable. To ensure it is not wasted, we all have a "check and balance" system. If what you are doing seems like a good idea in your mind, if it benefits not only you but others and feels good in your heart, and if it also stirs and nourishes your soul, I guarantee it is time well spent!

Time and space are all relative with the most influence, to the perspective of the matter in the focal point. So wherever you are and whatever it is that you do, do it well. Because you are always in the right spot at the right time for the person that needs you, whether *you* know it or not!

Everyone has heard the sayings "a penny for your thoughts" and "a picture is worth a thousand words." However, if you are *not* willing to listen or to take the time to look, you will never get your money's worth and will always be left with nothing to say.

We cannot alter, change, or suspend time, although we can learn to exercise patience in our endeavors and waiting, which empowers us in a small way to *control* time.

Time is so precious. We know in a day, there is not enough to accomplish all that we would like. When we give time in service of others, we freely give away one of our most precious commodities. Whether you give your time to assist your favorite charity, to help a friend or neighbor, or to do a simple act of kindness to a stranger, you give a gift that is precious; and I promise that is time *well* spent!

What is history but a small unit with which to measure time? If you unleash your entire treasure chest of God-given talents, tireless effort, and endless love into it, then and only then is born a tiny moment of everlasting greatness, a moment that, in itself, has the potential to forever change a life—yours or perhaps the life of someone else—and you may never even know it at the time.

America—the only place on earth where people can dream out loud and have the freedom to wander without restrictions, freely speak about, and chase after their dream, as well as have the time, resources, education, and technology available to them to catch it! The only thing needed is the individual imagination, determination, time, and hard work to invest to make your dreams a reality!

If we put all the extra time we felt we had in a quart mason jar, I doubt any of us would even fill the jar. Yet if all the time we had wasted were put in a pantry, it would be filled with quart mason jars clear full of time. If only there were a way we could reverse the two.

There never seems to be enough time to do everything we want to do on any given day. There is, however, always enough time to smile while we are not doing it.

Time. As the new week starts, we will rush to work; rush to meet deadlines; hurry to wait on customers; race to meet production schedules; fly to get children to school, practices, rehearsals, games, and friends and fly to pick them up; scramble to get breakfasts or dinners made; run to the store; jump for the phone; and I hope, make time for ourselves—time to slowly enjoy a cup of coffee or quietly sit down and read a good book or meditate; time to relax in a nice long bath, enjoy a gentle massage, or just kick back and enjoy memories of good times with family and friends in a softly lit room. I also hope we make time to get a good night's sleep so that we have the energy to get up and do it all over again.

"Whatever you are, be a good one" and "99.5 percent won't do" are sayings I like, which means to me that I must give 100 percent all the time to my every endeavor!

Time, whether measured digitally, mechanically, atomically, or through nature by the sun, moon, stars, and passing of the seasons, has one thing that is a constant factor: it never stops for anyone or anything!

Time never stops. Your watch may need winding. Your clock may need a battery. However, the clock of life is always charged. Life happens without any notice, without any alarms to wake you or to get you to move with it. This we must do on our own. If successful, we progress happily with time. If not, time passes us by, and we wonder where it went!

The people we give the majority of our time to are the ones who end up with the capability to hurt our hearts the most, and those who do are the ones who leave the deepest scars.

The simple truth is everyone lies or flirts with the truth. The question is, how big are the lies that you are willing to put up with? Don't expect of others a higher level of honesty than you are willing to hold yourself accountable.

No matter how much money you have or make, it will never be enough until you find a place in your heart that you are willing to be content with and not continue to want more and more and more.

There may never be enough time to do all we want. However, there is always enough time to do all that we can accomplish with love.

When you earn a dollar, it's easy to spend, it's harder to save, and it's even harder to give away. However, when opportunity presents itself, if you choose to give it to another, it will be the greater investment and the dollar that puts the biggest smile and warmest feeling in your heart.

Nearly everything in the world can be purchased if you have enough money. However, all the money in the world cannot buy a person honor, integrity, or trust of others. These can only be earned.

A time to do this, a time to do that, a time to look forward, and a time to look back. A time for reflection, a time to assess but never the time to get enough rest.

Tick tock, tick tock, time moves forward; it never stops. When it seems we can't keep up or can't keep track, it's because instead of looking forward, we're looking back.

Perception is a funny thing. Every now and then, we come across someone we think really needs our help. Usually, the timing isn't the best, and after a quiet grumble, we tend to lend a helping hand. Funny thing is when the deed is said and done and we realize how good we now feel, then comes the realization of who was really helped—that the real angel was one we asked for.

Every day you will leave a mark of some kind on the world and those with whom you interact. Your conduct and integrity will be a deciding factor on how the world will view your mark. Decide everyday if you want to leave behind strokes of crude graffiti or a brilliant piece of artwork for others to admire throughout your lifetime.

Piggy bank

Be prepared. The question is not if, but rather when you will have a financial emergency; and no matter the size of your piggy bank, the crisis will always be just a little bigger than your piggy.

When an elderly couple was once asked how they managed to stay together for sixty-five years, the old woman replied, "*We were born in a time where if something was broke, you fixed it—not throw it away!*"

—Unknown

I guess when it comes down to it, everything happens for a reason. So smile through your tears, laugh at your pain and love what you have, not what you want.

—Jill Coombs

SECTION FOUR

Love

Every heart sings a song, incomplete, until another heart whispers back. Those who wish to sing always find a song. At the touch of a lover, everyone becomes a poet.

—Plato

Love

Love—if it is not unconditional you have mistaken it for something else.

True love is found not where bodies physically collide but rather where hearts and souls entwine.

"What goes around comes around" is usually a saying associated in a negative light, or as a saying of revenge. However, just think what a wonderful saying and thing it would be if "what goes around" *started* with *love*!

Sometimes on the darkest of nights, the light of love can be found shining brightest from the eyes of a dear friend sent to light your path.

The heart of a loved one may be a great distance away with your eyes open, but close them, and you can almost feel their heart beat next to yours.

If you are determined to see things begin and end with love, the filling in between can be nothing but wonderful.

Love knocks or calls, often when you least expect it, and quietly and gently comforts you like a warm blanket on a chilly morning. It gives and takes but is not selfish in that it never takes more than it gives, when it is both given and received first from your heart.

LOVE = Listening openheartedly very essential

With today's technology, almost everything is available at the push of a button—and available in literally seconds, which most complain about if the download takes much longer than that. However, there is one thing that has its own clock, keeps its own time, cannot be forced, rushed, or hurried along. Though it can move in an instant, it moves at its own desired tempo, fast or slow. No matter the speed, if you wait for it to download, you will never be disappointed and will have to share its news with others immediately! What is it? Love! And it is compatible for download with every single style, make, and model of heart on the market, no matter the age or operating system!

Few definitions of *convenience* in the dictionary is "anything that adds to one's comfort," "personal well-being," "personally favorable condition," or "*saves work.*" When it comes to relationships the *best ones* are not convenient. You must always put some effort, work, and time with love if you hope to see it through to the "happily ever after."

What makes people gravitate toward others that they would like to be around? If you take a closer look, I believe you will find it is *not* money, stocks, or large estates. I believe you will find it is laughter, kindness, and love.

Most everything a person owns can be taken from them. However, memories and love locked in your heart, not a single soul can steal.

How would you explain the beautiful smell of a rose to someone who could not smell? Or describe the magnificent array of colors in a brilliant sunset to one who has never had sight? How would you relate the sweet taste of sugar to one that has never tasted it? I believe not all things that touch our hearts need words to pass them long. Some things are best conveyed with a simple hug, a tender touch, or an "I love you"!

Hearts in love do not like to be apart. However, if they must, one of love's comforting qualities is knowing that the special one you are away from, no matter how near or far, is missing you as you miss them, and that knowledge puts a great, big smile on your face, just as it does that special one, who is thinking of you even as you are thinking of them.

Everyone wants to be loved, but few are willing to remove the barriers around their hearts so that they might be filled with love! As long as the fear of getting hurt is greater than your ability to trust someone with all your heart, you can never know true love, because true love doesn't come in bits and pieces.

The loving and unprejudiced heart can make the right decision long before the uneducated mind that waits without faith for facts.

Love—if it is not unconditional, you have mistaken it for something else.

You don't have to count true friends using your fingers. Their names are already etched on the walls in your heart!

"Things that matter . . . things which don't." No matter how many lists or revisions of lists I make, when you get right down to it, life is all about people and our interactions with them (Loved ones, friends, and neighbors). Want to be rich? Love and take care of all of them.

Trust is the cornerstone of any relationship. In a business deal or a passionate love, there has to be trust at the foundation. Otherwise, the business deal will fall through or the fire of love will burn out. The best we can do is to be honest in all our affairs, business or love. It won't soften the pain if the other party does wrong, but at least you will have the satisfaction of knowing that you did not throw a stone at a glasshouse.

Some "hurts" you just can't fix for others. You can't wrap them, splint them, or find a Band-Aid or roll of gauze big enough to cover them.

For these "hurts," like a broken heart, the best you can do is to put your arms around the person hurting and let a softly spoken word and your heartfelt love do what they can.

A heart filled with love gives off warmth that everyone can feel!

Every piece of a heart beats for someone. Only when you find *true* love will two hearts beat as one.

Everyone has a soul. However, until you find true love and happiness, you will not find your soul mate.

When true love melts two hearts into one, your romantic walks on heavenly beaches, beneath the omnipotent glow of a heavenly sun melting into a crystalline ocean with a golden hue, will indeed be the romantic walks of eternal lovers!

Sometimes the most powerful and remembered conversations between lovers are had when the heart speaks and the mouth is silent.

True love can be communicated through a hug, a kiss, the holding of a hand, or even just by looking into the eyes of the one you love.

Hearts can speak to one another in a long silence or a brief moment sentiments like "I love you," "I understand," "I care," "everything will be fine," and "I am here for you."

When you hear "I love you" from the one you love and get a tingle down your spine or some goose bumps or get giggly and tongue-tied, you are on the right path!

If you fought for it, it was worth defending. If you sweated for it, it was worth the hard work. If getting it caused you pain, it was worth the suffering. If your heart ached along the way and now is overflowing, it was worth every emotional tear shed to feel the passion of love. That it was hard makes the victory taste so sweet. If it came easy, with little or no effort at all, it has likely already been forgotten.

Love can be desired, sought after, chased, coaxed, persuaded, given, offered, or entrusted, but it cannot be bought!

Light always shines outward just as love begins from within, and its warmth and light projects outward for others to feel. The hotter the fire in your furnace, your heart, the hotter and further that heat and warm glow will emit for others to feel. There is only one way to stoke the fire in your heart. It has to begin with you. No matter your size, make, model, age, ailments, or handicaps, if you can't love and feel good about who you are in your own skin, your fire will never get stoked hot enough for others to feel. Love yourself. Feel good about the good things you do and qualities you have, and praise yourself. For when you are content and love yourself, that joy and glow will not only attract others to you, it will project a loving heat source that will help fuel the fire in the hearts of all those around you, and in return, the love they emit will continue to fuel your own. Love—it begins and ends from within you.

Love is not effortless. It takes work. Its passionate fire needs to be fed, or the flame will eventually burn out. But if tendered with care and nurtured, the flame will blaze furiously for eternity!

You have never truly lost something until you have lost something that can never be replaced, something that was not manufactured, not bought, that you fight with all that was within you to protect. These things are a precious few: a true love, a true friend, a dear relative, someone who has shared a traumatic event or special experience with you, a brother-in-arms, your faith, and *freedom*!

True love, like a very fine wine, becomes more exquisite and exotic as it ages if it is handled properly and with care.

Follow your heart, use common sense, and laugh often. Help someone along your path and pray hard. No matter the path you're traveling on, by doing these things out of pure love, you are bound to end up at a beautiful destination and enjoy the trip there as well.

The hearts of lovers are very fragile. They can withstand a lot of pain but not without leaving scars that never truly heal. Once hurt, the hurt never truly ever goes away. Handle them with care!

In broad daylight, an act of kindness and love can stick out like the glow as a lantern burning in the dark of night. Just as on a cold night, those same acts can give one the warmth of a summer sun.

For whatever reason, it is just a fact that there comes a time in our life when someone among those we love the most and hold dearly, we (most often unintentionally) will probably hurt the most. Whether by word or action, unintentional or not, we need to do all we can to correct, fix, and help heal the heart to whom we caused pain or sorrow. Life has a funny way of bringing everything full circle. One day, we will *all* be on the receiving end of the hurt. When that day comes, you will *not* want to be wishing that the person who caused your heart to ache will treat you better than you treated the person whose feelings or heart had a pain that you were responsible for.

An $8 flashlight, no matter how old, beat-up, cracked, dented, or rusty, with fresh batteries that projects light, is always more appreciated in a power outage than a brand-new $180 tactical flashlight with dead batteries. No matter your make, model, age, size, or condition, if you let your light shine bright, you will be loved and appreciated.

Love can make you feel giggly all over. Kind of like giggling after farting in a hot tub with the jets on and knowing that you are the only one that will ever know about it.

Love isn't always "Moonbeams and pixie dust" though it could be. Life isn't always "Brier patches and thistles" though you could let it be. True friends aren't waiting for you on every street corner, but they could seem that close. Every day will never be all smiles and laughs, but every day could be full of them both. One thing is for certain. Every day, life, love, and friendships, will give "Back to you," exactly what *you* put into them.

I believe to search for love one should start by trying to be a good friend to those who you find interesting with common likes and interests. A true love that will last is simply choosing a best friend that you want to share every moment and experience every day of your life with. Everything else, including the physical elements of a loving relationship, is just icing on the cake.

Love radiates for others to feel. The hotter the fire in your furnace, your heart, the hotter and further that heat will emit for others to feel. There is a way to stoke the fire in your heart. No matter your size, make, model, age, ailments or handicaps, if you can love and feel good about you, in your own skin, your fire will get stoked hot enough for others to feel. Love yourself. Feel good about the positive things you do, the good qualities you have and praise yourself. When you are content and love yourself, that joy and warm glow will attract others to you and project loving warmth that will fuel the fire in the hearts of others. In return the love they emit will continue to fuel your own. Love, it begins and ends with you.

Life and love waits for no-one. The sooner one decides what they want out of life, or who they want to share life with, and chases after it or them, the greater the odds for catching, having and enjoying. Don't let the fear of failing, or rejection cause you to hesitate and miss your golden moment. Go for it!

Love, when it comes to you in life, and you obtain it, takes work to maintain it. The more you give of yourself and work at it when you obtain it, the more you will appreciate it. You will be careful not to be careless and let it slip away. If you expect life to deliver love and happiness to your doorstep without working and giving of yourself for it, love will be a disappointment and happiness long sought after will never be won permanently.

Winged heart in healing

Ask not what your country can do for you—ask what you can do for your country.

President John F. Kennedy
January 20, 1961

SECTION FIVE

Volunteering

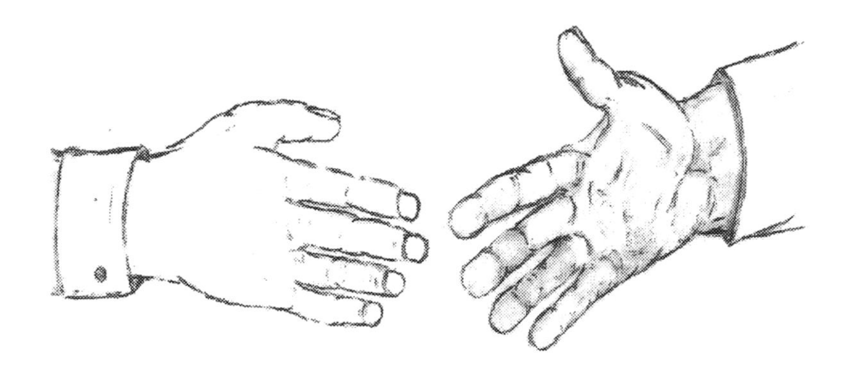

Volunteer hands

Random acts of kindness remind me of lightning: they often take but mere seconds to have a very powerful effect, are always impressive, can give you a chill that makes the hair on your neck stand up and warm your heart at the same time, and are always welcomed and refreshing, like a soft, gentle summer rain, which can follow lightning.

You may not get all you want out of life, but you can put everything you want into it, and if you do it with caring treatment of others in mind, you will get back more than your heart can hold, of the things in life that are really important!

If you have an ache you want to disappear, do something for someone else. Your ache will go away for a moment, and if only for a moment, it's a great moment.

No matter what group or organization you choose to volunteer in and give of your time, that "feel good" in your heart makes every second of that time priceless!

I may not hear birds sing anymore, but I hear every word someone speaks out of love. I may not see someone roll their eyes at me because I am slow to walk behind, but I see everyone that could use my help. I may not be able to feel my feet, but I can feel the warmth in my heart, which comes from helping others.

If you have to tell someone about everything you do for others, are you really doing those acts of charity to help others, or for your own self-gratification? True, selfless service is, more often than not, anonymous.

Seen an ad for sunless tanning today. I can Fake Bake my skin, dye my hair, or even change the colors of my eyes with contact lenses—all are temporary. Making a change that will make a difference must come from within, from your heart. If you want to really feel good and project a radiant glow that will get noticed, try a simple act of random kindness. The results will last longer than your fake tan.

There is a saying that says, "To change the world, you must start with yourself." I believe that. However, since 90 percent of Americans never travel outside America, let alone the state they live in, I say, why try to change the world? Why not first make a change in your own community! All it takes is a small investment of time to have a *big* impact!

Volunteerism, community involvement, and accountability of elected officials—too often I hear people complain about the way people are running their community. Yet a few gentle questions will reveal that the complainer did not vote, does not attend city council or town hall meetings, and is not involved in volunteering at all. Strong communities thrive upon involvement and participation from everyone!

It is fun to look for angels. They are quite easy to spot for me. The secret is not to look for wings but rather someone doing a kind deed.

Why? Because I can do it, because I want to, because I am free to do it, because it is the right thing to do and I will feel good doing it. Helping someone. Try it!

There is nothing quite like the sense of accomplishment from achieving a difficult or hard earned goal while volunteering.

Especially when during the pursuit of accomplishing it, you were told you would never be able to do it.

Volunteers perform their deeds with reverence and humility from the start; simply giving selfless service from their volunteering heart.

Some people tire their arms right out from patting themselves on the back and their mouths by telling everyone about the quarter they flipped to a homeless person—while someone else is exercising their fingertips, while listening to them, by writing themselves a note to stop and get a new coat on the way home, to replace the nice one they had on this morning that they generously gave to the same cold homeless man their coworker is still bragging about flipping the quarter to.

I am no stranger to pain, sorrow, or long-suffering. I have befriended sheer exhaustion, sleepless nights, and hunger. I have enjoyed the feeling of accomplishment of hard physical labor. I have fought for my country and for what I believe in. All have made me who I am. I hope now I have the tools I need to *not* be a stranger to the pain, sorrow, or suffering of others, and when opportunity allows, my toolbox will enable me to ease their pain or sorrows, or at least share them.

Believe it or not, there *is* a way that everyone can actually "see into the future." All one has to do is simply look into the eyes of someone that is really down on their luck that you opt to do a random act of kindness for. You will be able to see a soul that will truly be edified and full of gratitude well into the future for a very long time!

You can tell if your heart is in the right place by the occasional blister on your hands from helping others.

You can tell someone one hundred times that you care about them, and they may remember that you told them that five of those times. You can *do* something for someone in need, without being asked for help, just *acting* out of a pure kindness of heart, and they will not only *never* forget it, but odds are, they will not stop talking about it or telling others of your act of kindness. Actions really *do* speak louder than words!

It isn't about what you give but rather how and the spirit in which it is given. Many priceless and memorable gifts cost nothing to give: a smile, a wave, a hug, a few words of kindness from the heart—all priceless!

When you give from the heart, you don't look for a mention of it in the headlines of the newspaper. You'll feel your headline in the warmth of your soul and the peace in your mind.

Volunteers do their work for others. They do not seek attention or accolades galore. They simply do their work for peace of mind and for pride. They truly are never seeking anything more.

In a room full of healthy, fit people who are being loud, energetic, and full of spirit, zest, and zing, can a person walk in and simply say, "I need a couple of volunteers"? And instantly, the room will go quiet, people will slouch down in their chairs, coughing will become a common sound, and those on their feet will start limping to a chair to sit on (hee-hee). I think this is a tactic SWAT teams should deploy to send mobs of people running and quickly defuse a riot situation. They just simply need to pull out the bullhorn and yell, "I need a couple of volunteers." Before their very eyes, the angry mobs will suddenly disperse and vanish (ha-ha).

How do you spell *volunteer*? It's easy: L-O-V-E!

Volunteers understand it is not about simply giving a handout but rather giving a hand-up. It is those that need it that we need to teach to not be ashamed to take a helping hand up, get back on your feet, and next time, pay it forward and be the extended helping hand.

Nothing can make you feel more fresh and clean than the dirtiest hands and soiled clothes from rendering selfless service to someone who was really in need of help.

There will always be a place to stand for a willing volunteer to lend a helping hand.

Imagine finding a bottle on a beach. Imagine you rubbing it and a genie pops out. Now imagine the genie saying, "For releasing me, I will give to you ten times what you have given to others." Would you be any better off than you were before finding the bottle?

Often, one finds that by helping others, answers to some of your own problems seem to sprout up all around you.

There will always be a need, for a special, giving volunteer, to perform a special, kind, and loving deed.

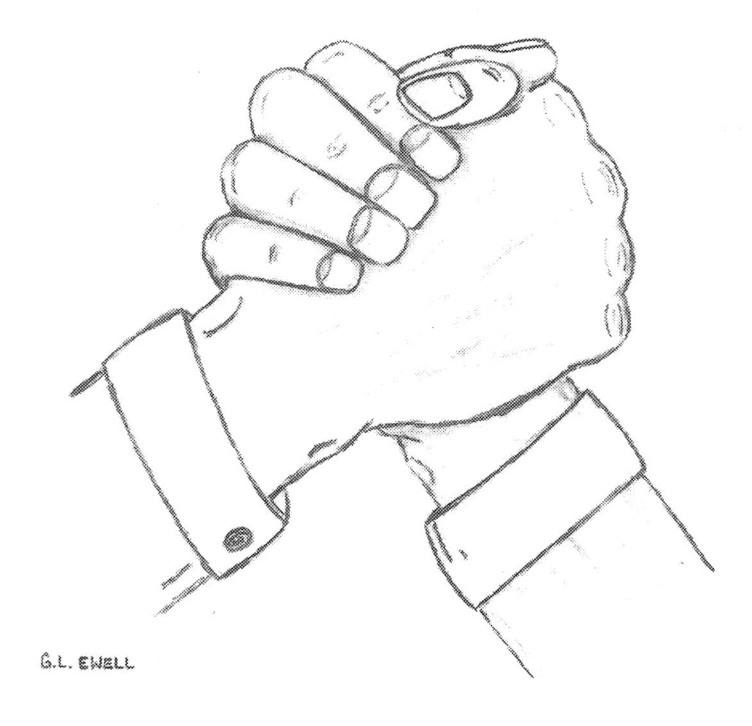

Bonding hands

When the people find they can vote themselves money; that will herald the end of the republic.

—Benjamin Franklin

SECTION SIX

Military, Government, and Government-Recognized Holidays

The Lincoln Memorial in Washington DC

Obviously, sketching faces is not my strength, help me out and exercise your imagination here. Please note, the quote by President Lincoln above is a quote of his I like. It is not inscribed anywhere on or within the actual memorial temple to which his memory is enshrined.

We live in the greatest country in the world not because we have better ideas, imaginations, aspirations, or hopes and dreams than other people in the world do but rather because we have the fertile fields of freedom in our country to plant those seeds in. God bless America!

There is no tapestry in the world more skillfully and carefully woven with ethnicity, heritage, racial tolerance, religious expression, individual emotion, intellectualism, compassion, freedom, and love than the alluring beauty of the tapestry of Americana! Woven within it is a very small but ever so strong thread that holds it all tightly together. That thread is called *vetarans*!

I want to say thank you to everyone who has stood by their defender of freedom. I want to say thank you to everyone who has supported a family member, who has worn the uniform of a defender of freedom. Thank you to *anyone* who supports our defenders of freedom and appreciates the sacrifices they and their families make. I will remember each of you as well!

There are so many young soldiers with such serious and permanent injuries and scars of war to cope with for the rest of their lives. Indeed, all gave some, some gave all, and some are still giving!

Our great and very young nation rose with light speed to become the dominant world leader only because our Founding Fathers were divinely inspired to set up a government of its people, for the people, and gave people the freedom to allow them to pursue their dreams, invent and create whatever their hearts and minds desired. Too bad so many creative and genius minds are perverted and use their freedom to invent evil ways to corrupt minds, cheat, steal, defraud, and promote pornography. If all *those* combined talents were able to focus on the good for humanity, we would probably already have a cure for cancer, more balanced ecosystems, a way to make ocean water useable for drinking and irrigation of agricultural crops, and cleaner air.

A day from hell, the Twin Towers fell. A terrorist attack, like a knife in the back. So much bloodshed, so many loved ones dead. The entire nation did unite, we sent our soldiers to fight. Congress declared war so this could happen no more upon our shores. So when the sun went down on the East Coast and West, our citizens would know they could peaceably rest. Today, remember the fallen heroes from that day and our soldiers who are still in harm's way.

We all have had our hard times. Been down on our luck. If you happen to get down on your luck, don't forget to remind yourself that at least you are in *America*! Beats being down in Somalia, where I am not sure it would be a good place to be up on your luck!

Think of how peaceful and safe our neighborhoods, communities, and cities would be, of how many needless laws would not have to be passed, enforced, and regulated; the revenue that is legislating and enforcing these needless laws could be saved if only everyone would regulate themselves as strictly as they desire to regulate and control everyone around them.

With *voter* turnout percentages so low in the last election, it makes me sick that we take for granted this freedom that our Founding Fathers fought for so fervently. The unemployment rate is so high. I hope in this next election the numbers will dramatically increase. Everyone that is unemployed should have plenty of time to vote. Anyone unemployed that doesn't vote doesn't deserve a job!

Why is it when the government is always in a financial crisis, you never hear politicians say we will have to cut back on aid to foreign countries, negotiate and refinance loans borrowed from other countries, cut back on humanitarian projects our military is scheduled to do, or stop funding contracts that are no longer needed to support a war that's mission has changed? Instead, they just scare the elderly, the disabled, the veterans, and the soldiers who are still in harm's way. Use your power to vote and vote wisely come election time.

People complain about taxes, "Obama-care" and gun control. Yet, there is less than a thirty percent voter "turn out" during elections. What is there to complain about? We are getting the exact amount of representation, government control and regulation that we are allowing. If you really want to see a change, then rally, get involved and vote! We are getting exactly what we allow. It is a government "Of the People," remember? We decide who the government leaders are by voting. Instead of complaining, stay informed, communicate with your elected officials, attend your city council meetings, and town hall meetings and most of all, get out and vote!

It is a fact that stupid laws get passed, often because a small minority of village idiots is smart enough to come together, unite, pester their congressional representative, and vote. All while the majority sit back, do nothing, and are absent from the polling booths at home, saying "Hell, that will never pass!" When it does, then who are the village idiots! Get out and vote!

"How little do my countrymen know what precious blessings they are in possession of, and which no other people on earth enjoy" *Thomas Jefferson*. If that is what he thought during his time, I imagine he would really be disgusted with his fellow *countrymen* today. I am just thinking out loud again.

A wounded warrior suffers far greater from mental injuries than physical ones. The physical injuries are just daily mental reminders to the soldiers that they can no longer be the soldiers or persons they were before the injury, a reminder that they will never be the same for themselves or their families. Therein lies the new battle redefining the new soldier.

While the last of our combat soldiers have left Iraq, let us not forget that over one hundred thousand are in Afghanistan, still fighting the war on terrorism. Moms, dads, husbands, wives, sons, and daughters are still in harm's way, doing their duty and missing the comforts of home and their families and loved ones so that we can *all* enjoy spending every precious minute we can with ours!

Tonight, I will not complain about the pain in my legs, as my friend who lost his would love to feel my pain. I won't complain about my bed now, rather smile, remembering I didn't have to hand-sweep sand off it before getting in. In the morning, I won't complain if I can't sleep in; rather, I will be grateful I don't need to check my boots for scorpions before I put my feet in them. I'll enjoy a sunrise without the sound of mortar rounds nearby. I'll say a prayer for my military brothers and sisters who are still in harm's way.

Think of the world we would live in today if our Founding Fathers did not have ironclad guts, nerves of steel, strong moral fiber, and wisdom to seek the divine help of our Creator, as they—outnumbered in resources, supplies, and people—prepared to take on, stand up to, and break away from the most powerful monarchy in the world! God bless those who have followed and still today are protecting the precious gift of freedom they gave us.

There are politicians who want to cut veteran benefits. Currently, only 2 percent to 4 percent of the population of America has ever served in the military (use whichever stat you want). Of that small percentage, one out of five suicides every day in America is a military service member. If politicians want to cut veteran benefits so badly, all they need to do is the pathetic—*nothing*! The alarmingly high suicide rate will cut the budget for them. Our veterans deserve better than *nothing*!

Today, Independence Day, as I humbly look upon every flag I see, I will solemnly look upon the beautiful stars on a sea of blue and remember that across an ocean, men and women from every star (state) on the flag are protecting my freedom. I will see the red stripes and know blood is shed by many protecting me. I will see the white stripes and know that peace will be prayed for this day, by soldiers, as well as by me, for us at home and them abroad!

The week of February fourteenth each year is designated as National Salute to Hospitalized Veterans Week. It is an opportunity for America to say thank you to the more than ninety-eight thousand men and women who are cared for daily at VA medical facilities across the country. If you can't find time to visit a VA medical center, not a problem. You can do something even simpler to honor this special group of Americans. Each time you see a flag this week, think of a freedom you enjoy. Then with your heart and mind, just simply whisper, "Thank you."

The seventh day of August each year has been set aside as "National Purple Heart Remembrance Day." The "Purple Heart" is a medal that soldiers do not seek to earn. For those who have received one, it is most likely a moment in time they wish they could forget. It was a moment in time where seconds felt like minutes, minutes felt like hours, and hours felt as though they would never end. It was a moment of time that for many, compared to the situation they were in, hell would have seemed like a nice spot for a vacation. Many others gave their all and the medal was presented to loved ones they left behind. To the men and women who have received this medal, I salute you for your courage and sacrifice. I also humbly shed tears in remembrance of every drop of blood that you shed, for the freedoms that I enjoy and the country that I love.

I remind myself everyday not to take for granted the luxuries we all enjoy, that those protecting our freedoms are without. Some of our military service members have been without these luxuries for nearly a year. It is not big things I mean either. It is the little things we don't appreciate. Things like not hand sweeping a layer of dust and sand off our beds before we climb into them and our bare feet on carpet that is void of scorpions and camel spiders. A bathroom ten steps, not 100 yards, from our beds and not shared by 300 other people and we don't have to pack a machine gun to it. It is clean civilian clothes. It is private personal space and time. I can have a slice of fresh pizza, with real toppings, a glass of milk and water I dare drink. I can go to sleep on a quiet night without the sound of gunfire, rockets or mortar rounds. It is a bath, a beer, and lights that do not fade bright and dim with the surge of a generator or the noise of one. I can go to stores with anything I want or need in them. I can see friends and family anytime I want. For the smallest of our luxuries, someone has and continues to pay a price for them. May God bless those, protecting our blessings and us to not take them for granted.

I just came in from outside, saying goodnight to Old Glory after her special day. "The land of the free and the home of the brave," the *depth* of *all* that she stands for, two thirds of the world's population will never have a clue, never understand, or ever get a taste of in their entire life. For the love, honor, and privilege of being an American, I thank you, God!

Thank you to all those who have endured cold, dark nights in Europe's black forests, the bitter bite of a Korean winter, the damp, endless rains of Vietnam, the jungle and humidity of the islands in the Pacific, the heat of Africa and Somalia, the terrain of Afghanistan, and the blasting sandstorms of Iraq—and done it in battle—I salute you! Thank you all for your courage and selfless sacrifices.

Imagine if the patriotism that people exhibited on Independence Day, they showed every day of the week. If only people would want to feed the hungry and homeless every day, like they do wanting to donate their time or money, to ensure charity organizations serve them a Thanksgiving meal. What if everyone displayed the kindness to "pan handlers" every day, like they do the day before Christmas? Imagine if everyone acted all week long, like they do on Sunday, what a difference it would make in our country! If only people would act every day of the week, like they have shown they can act for just one day! Just imagine . . .

It is a shame you never hear real news on the news! We don't need more laws in America. What we need are more men to take a stand for what is right and protect their families. We need more citizens with the moral courage to get involved and do the right thing no matter how big or small the problem in our neighborhoods and cities rather than turning a blind eye to the problems, pretending that they will just go away. That is my opinion anyway.

We have all heard "When in Rome, do as the Romans would do." I say wherever you are in the world do what is in your heart and do what is right! Perhaps that is what is wrong with Congress. Instead of doing the right thing for America, they are too busy trying to "do as the Romans" they replaced when elected.

It is a fact that a donkey can be one of the most stubborn animals on the planet. It is also a fact that an elephant has one of the smallest brains, in ratio to its size, of any animal on the planet. Of all the magnificent creatures that could represent strength, loyalty, power, protection and pride, our leaders chose a donkey and an elephant to represent their political parties. I now know where the term "Dumb-Ass" originated! Coincidently, it would appear as if they picked right. This is because most of the legislation that is important for America does not get acted upon. Why is this? It seems to me that one party is too stupid and the other too stubborn to work together for the good of the people! However, this is just my opinion (ha, ha).

Today another soldier died, leaving behind a weeping spouse, child, mother, father, sibling or friend. Let them not weep alone. Remember those who are in harm's way and their families. They are giving their all so that we may enjoy the peace and joy of this holiday within the borders of our great nation.

Sleep did not come again tonight. Though I do not hear the war anymore, I still *see* it, even with just one eye. I see faces twisted up with pain, heartache, exhaustion and fear. I see faces with the never ending stare of death upon them. Guess I'll go start coffee. Today is a new day and a chance to see the glass half-full rather than half-empty.

Last year, for the second year in a row, soldier suicides killed more of our servicemen and women than the enemy did. While my own post-traumatic stress syndrome and petty problems kept me up all night again, at least one of my brothers or sisters had demons that drove them to commit suicide. Today I will thank my Creator that my demons were kept at bay and pray that today, someone will notice a soldier in distress.

The war on terrorism has become the longest war in American history. Longer than the Civil War and World War II combined.

Over twelve years of sustained war has taken a toll on our military. Suicide has taken twice as many lives as the enemy has. Our military service members need our help and support. We cannot allow this trend to continue. You can support our military service members even if you disagree with the war. Soldiers follow orders. Hold the people accountable who are giving them, our President and Congress.

As Thanksgiving is approaching, everyone becomes more conscious of things they are thankful for that are not usually pondered on much prior to the holiday. I suspect this is true of all living things. In fact, I believe the happy-go-lucky turkey who has been haphazard in communion with his Creator is now feverishly in prayer thanking him for vegetarians!

With Veterans Day over, this morning there are approximately thirty million turkeys trying their very best to walk like a duck.

I think I will petition my congressman to introduce a bill to make December the National Thesaurus Month. I laugh my butt off watching people try to come up with politically correct ways to wish each other a merry Christmas, without actually saying "Christmas." While I ponder more about how to word my letter to my congressman, have a very merry Christmas everyone!

I am surprised that someone has not tried to sue the government for discrimination over Valentine's Day; claiming that our kidneys, liver, lungs, brain and other organs need a day they can be celebrated like the heart. (ha, ha)

The truth is there is no peace on earth, though we would like there to be. But thank God, through his grace and in part to the security our armed forces are providing for us in America and others around the globe, there is some *peace* in which we *can* enjoy the love of family, friends, and the *reason* we celebrate our Christmas holiday.

Yesterday I saw a store already putting out a Christmas display. I swear the commercialism of the holiday starts earlier every year. While I would prefer to hand out some Halloween candy and enjoy a Thanksgiving dinner before I see a Christmas tree, there isn't a day in the year that's not appropriate to thank our Creator for the blessings and freedoms we enjoy being Americans!

As we enjoy our holiday, someone has set an empty plate for their loved one a world away, who spent it in combat boots on patrol today, protecting those they love, those around them, and the civilians they pass along their way, and of course, all the reasons we give thanks to a higher power on this day. Others have set an empty plate for their soldier who nevermore will be present to eat what loving hands made. So for them, I ask humbly that sometime today, in your heart, you will briefly say a quick thanks, remembering them with your loved ones, to those who protect freedom' s flame.

With time for reflection between now and the New Year, I am amazed at all that has happened in world history this year. Throughout the world, the United States, our military and humanitarian relief organizations have made monumental footprints to help, aid, assist, and provide security for people that will be forever etched in history, and they can only be labeled as great works. I hope the New Year will be one that we all hold our Congressional delegates responsible for putting into motion that which is within their power to ensure great works are performed for those needing relief within our own borders, as well as abroad.

As long as there is communism, dictators, and tyranny in the world, there will be enslaved and oppressed people, markets, and exchange rates; unregulated, unfair, and unsafe trade and commodities; and jealousy and hatred for the United States of America by world leaders whose own people will try desperately to get free of the reign of terror they live under and try to get to America, as well as terrorists trying to mastermind attacks on America. All of which means the American soldier will *always* have a post to pull a guard duty during Christmas. This holiday, I am ever grateful for our servicemen and women on duty and the families who support them and will have an empty seat set at their holiday dinner table in memory of their absent loved one.

M1A1 Abrams battle tank

American soldiers don't fight because they hate what's in front of them . . . they fight because they love what's behind them.

—Unknown

Within all of us, each and every human being is the power to heal—to heal ourselves as well as others. It is however, left to each of us alone to figure out how to access, and administer these powerful resources within us all, for our own healing and the healing of others.

—Gordon L. Ewell

SECTION SEVEN

Spiritual Help and Self-Help

Iron cross

Wouldn't it be something if people tried to get as close to their God in times of happiness and joy as they do in times of despair, crisis, and death?

I believe that a person's true honor and strength of character will someday be measured by their actions when they thought no one was watching them!

There is but one thing greater than America and the people blessed to live here . . . and that is the Almighty God responsible for the creation of both!

You will run into danger on any path you choose to travel in life. No matter which path you are on, take big steps or little ones, but take each step with faith, not fear, in any direction you wish to travel.

Within us all is the ability to unlock the countless opportunities that are tucked inside the rising sun of each bright new day! However, it is up to each of us to remember where we put they key to the lock.

This week, I will commit to the person in my mirror that I will use my sight to look for someone in need, my strength to perform a kind little deed, my heart to show compassion, my mind to think good thoughts, and my knees to thank my Creator for each of these gifts.

It is an easy thing for me to say that my world shrunk when I became handicapped and housebound. It is easy to make jokes about it when friends are around or on the phone. It is a very different and difficult thing to accept when I am all alone and a heart and mind want to travel and explore the world that is no longer accessible to me.

With the coming of each new dawn, I have the knowledge that I and only I have the potential to look it right in the eye and unlock its omnipotent energy to make this day *great* for me!

Honesty, integrity, and valor: if we would make these three characteristics the armor, shield, and sword we put on every day, we would find we could walk tall with our head held high and be full of courage and pride. We would also find more honesty in all our dealings with others and realize, if everyone did this, we could drop the sword and shield, as there would probably be few battles left to fight.

When anniversaries that hit hard come along, no matter how fervently you try to hide them, they will not subside until they want to, which is about the same time you are willing to let them slide through your exhausted fingers, of a once tightly closed fist that held them, for another year.

"There is no such thing in anyone's life as an unimportant day" (Alexander Woolcott, American writer). This is so true. More often than not, those whom we make the most impact on have *not* had our focused attention. However, we have theirs!

I love the way everything smells after it rains. Everything is fresh and clean! It is a lot like a good cry! It cleanses the soul and heart, leaving everything fresh and clean and ready for a new start!

Life is definitely what we choose to make of it! However, before you criticize someone too harshly, remember that we are not all born blessed with the same ingredients to start baking our birthday cake with!

Honesty—you can teach it, preach it, judge and chastise those you believe are not, confront, and even point out to others someone whom you catch in a lie. However, until you can first enact it, practice it, and judge yourself by the same standard you hold others to, every step you take is continuing down a dishonest path!

Live your life like a tightrope walker in a circus. However, be the tightrope walker with the courage and unwavering belief in yourself that you take each step without fear or worry about a safety net below.

Some days, all that motivates me is the knowledge that I had better not complain, because I know others in situations far worse. I also know they do not complain near as much as some who have things a hundred times better off than they do. Their example humbles me. It is a reminder that I only need to focus on myself and not judge others on either side of the pendulum from where I am.

When my world comes crashing down upon me, I'd like to think I will have the optimism to say, "Dang, if the stars aren't so amazingly more omnipotent and absolutely stunning being this much closer to them!"

Everyone on the planet is handicapped or disabled. Some physically, some mentally, some when it comes to love, some spiritually. And others handicapped without the common sense or humility to *not* make fun of or show compassion toward those who are truly suffering from a handicap or disability!

Pain is Pain and it all hurts. Some pains longer than others. For physical and mental pain, the body can heal and modern medicine or holistic medicinal practices and drugs can help speed recoveries and healing time. But for heartache, there are no Band-Aids. So remember the hurt. That way, you can be sure your actions are not the source of a pain that will not heal for someone else.

"Duty, honor, country" is not just some cheesy slogan. It is a way of life for men of honor and character.

Life can throw a lot of unexpected curves at a person. In the baseball game of life, we can all hit a home run. However, to hit one, you have to make the effort to swing the bat. While in life's batter's box, when you are at the plate, look the pitcher right square in the eye. When he delivers it, don't be afraid to swing at a well-thrown curveball. It just may be the pitch you hit a home run with!

Letters by themselves are hardly noticeable. Properly paired and linked together, they become words and have meaning. Words assembled together in the right order become sentences; having behind them definition, depth, and meaning can promote healing to the sick, start a revolution, or break a lover's heart. We have the power to assemble our words for good or bad every single day.

I was thinking of a list of most powerful weapons. I think these are top of my list: the sharpest weapon is the tongue, the most powerful and mighty is the pen, the best shield is a memory, and the most efficient is a helping hand. We all have them and can decide whether we use our weapons to do good works or to cause harm.

The school of hard knocks is one I believe we all have attended and earned a certificate of completion from. Or if you are like me, you went back and, through further life studies, have continued on and got a master's degree. Fortunately, most of life's lessons learned are like a bad haircut. For instance, if you make a bad decision, it normally just takes a few days of personal growth to get looking and feeling good again.

I was blessed to see the world while I was in great health. Further, I could easily travel and get about with complete freedom and unrestricted mobility. Now with some severe impairments, due to being blown up at war, I have been even more blessed. For now, I am able to see the world through the eyes of hardship, which is how the majority of the world's population has to wake up and view their corner of the world every day! I am blessed to be able to have my eye opened to a reality that has changed my view for the better and increased my perception, appreciation, and empathy with people and things that surround me every day!

A wish for peace, for just a day, that there would be no rocket's red glare, no mortars exploding or roadside bombs, and no hail of gunfire. A wish that for a day, the only sounds to be heard are the silence of peace, the laughter of friends and family, and the hope that chimes through the eyes of a child, living a day without fear.

The secret to happiness: it's honesty. If everyone were honest with themselves, their partners, their friends, their business dealings, and their Creator, everything else would fall into place perfectly! We would still have our hardships, but we could work through them . . . honestly!

The heart is a barometer for the soul. You can bet if there is a low pressure system in the heart—some guilt, a sorrow, or coldness—there is sure to be a storm in the soul.

If first we asked, "How will it affect others?" rather than "How will it benefit me?" we would find, by default, we would benefit by the results of our sincere answers and actions.

No matter what kind of a stumble or fall you take in life, whether it is a mental, spiritual, or an actual physical fall, if you keep getting up and challenging yourself, I guarantee, nothing but good will come out of it!

I wonder why, with the millions of copies that have been printed, you will never find Bible on any book lists, like as one of the best-selling books of all time!

As none of us are perfect, we are bound to make mistakes, use poor judgment, do or say something we regret that hurts someone we care about, or just plain do something dumb. These actions themselves are not all bad. What makes them so is if we fail to forgive ourselves or others, ask for forgiveness, or learn from our mistakes and *continue* to make the *same* mistakes.

Don't wait until the New Year to resolve to be a better person. The season is upon us now that people need you to be the best you that you can and give from your heart, your wallet, or the sweat of your brow.

The toughest of men, the baddest of the bad, those who fear nothing more than defeat, achieve their victories in part because they do not forget their Creator and seek his presence in battle, to free the oppressed and for the good of humanity.

No matter how physically banged up, damaged, or broken you are on the outside, or how angry, sad, confused, and full of heartache you are on the inside, when you put your mind to giving help, aid, or comfort or uplifting others, you will find your ailments will disappear. You will feel good inside and out. You will even find a smile has landed upon your face. Even if the moment is short-lived, it is a great short moment.

Compliments are wonderful and underused tools for instant and positive attitude changes. They also can instantly flip the switch on someone's smile button. Often, while I am at the store checkout register, being often slow, I can see the look of "Why did I pick this line" on the people behind me. A simple compliment of "Thank you for your patience with me, I know I am slow" will replace a scorned look of "This is killing me" with a smile and often a reply of "Oh no, you are just fine, I am not in any hurry at all." A little positive communication can indeed change the world, or at least your little corner of it.

It is almost impossible to have negative thoughts and smile and to be angry while laughing. If everyone could pass a little something on to just one person every day, to make them smile or laugh, what an impact it would have. Too bad weapons of war could not shoot people with smiles or blast them with laughter. I hope all of you get to enjoy *both* today!

You can always find both good and bad in things readily every day if you look for them. People have a tendency to think you *always* have to look for the good. I say, perspective being everything, that often it pays to look for the *bad*. You'll never find problems skipping daily through a field of daisies. Sometimes, you have to dig among thistles to uproot them. If you catch the *bad* before it has time to take root, you just may be able to make it something *good* of it.

Precious memories bring us joy and peace of mind. They also have a direct link to the heart. More often than not, the link between heart and mind is tears. They enrich a memory, happy or sad, so should they flow, don't suppress them. Rather let them flow and be blessed by the depth of feeling they add to those precious memories.

When all else seems to fail, make a call! Call home, phone a friend, dial a crisis hotline. There is *always* someone who wants to hear from you; one person in particular, and the communication line is *always* open! To access it, all you have to do is open your heart and take a knee.

We can choose to run through life with blinders on, having tunnel vision as life blows by us. Or we can choose to open the door on all our senses, open our minds, our hearts, view and interact with the entire world around us, and truly enjoy the glory and all the wonders this life offers us every day.

Everything and everyone evolves with time in one form or another. We make New Year's resolutions in part to evolve and become a better us. It is funny, however, that just as we seem to know what is best for us, life will throw us a curveball out of nowhere, and we will have to make a transformation to adapt to the new road placed before us if we desire to be successful.

With the changing of the season, a calmer climate and more gentle and stable weather will come. This ironically is exactly what I seek to self-improve in myself: a calmer, more gentle, and more stable me.

It is said that one definition of *hell* is when "the man you are meets the man you *could* have been." For this severely wounded warrior, my hell began when the man I am was looking into the mirror and tried to remember the man who he was! I am not sure who I was then or who I'll be tomorrow, but I know I'll be better off, if I treat people with kindness *today*!

The war on terrorism has taken a tremendous toll on so many. Not just in soldier lives that have been directly or indirectly lost (giving the ultimate price for freedom) but also with the wounded, families, and caregivers as well. In my own case, I was severely wounded. However, *not* totally disabled. Rather, I was given an opportunity from a higher power to enjoy seeing life from a different point of view.

Sometimes it is not possible or conceivable to let go of fear that a person may have about any given event, activity or circumstance they might find themselves in. It is however, possible to turn that fear into a positive energy that can help you stay focused, alert, and achieve the outcome you desire; no matter how easy or difficult the task.

In your light, dear God, allow me to learn from my past and apply it to my future. I'll strive to be a better man tomorrow than today, that I may rest easier tonight.

In life, there is a balance in all things. Today, there will be, for everyone who chooses to look, a dozen reasons to smile, laugh out loud, and be happy and content. There will also be a hundred reasons to get angry on the morning commute, be upset with coworkers, and be agitated with endless demands from others that seem to leave no time for one's own personal needs. Yet within us all lies the freedom of letting our hearts see that which brings it joy, or our minds embrace the garbage of others' actions, which by design overshadows the natural beauties of the little things that can make every day special.

No one wanders this world alone. For wherever the adventurous heart dares travel, highest mountain top, hottest desert, ocean floor, thickest jungles or the stars, I believe a celestial guide is always close at hand and ready to act, if called upon.

Today, the same two roads greet me. I can choose to let my aches, pains, and things I have lost bog me down and drag me down the path of self-pity; or I can choose to be grateful for *what* and *who* I have in my life and travel the other path, where I know I can always find a treasure along the way. It's time to paint on a smile and start looking for treasure.

Everyone has heard "it is always darkest before the storm." A good time to buy flashlight batteries is on a sunny day. But in case you forget and a storm hits, don't forget there is always a light you can turn on. To access the switch is easy: simply take a knee.

If the majority of people would *act* all week long like they do on Sunday, the world would be a wonderfully different place to live in.

When the road ahead appears to be all uphill, don't get discouraged. Rather, keep reminding yourself of how beautiful and majestic the view will be when you get to the summit!

Some of the world's most beautiful flowers bloom from the most obnoxious weeds. I guess we sometimes just need to have the patience to grow through some of life's unpleasantness to get to a point where we can enjoy our own beautiful bloom.

From the humble heart of a broken ol' warrior, I am grateful for the peace of this day and grateful for the honor I have of calling you *all* friends! I thank God for America, for the freedom we enjoy, for those bravely protecting both, and pray I *never* take either for granted!

All things change but one. Times change, the seasons change, and people and things age, and as all do, there remains one constant: God's love. It can be found in all time, in any season, available to all people, and it never dims.

I could easily cheat you or tell you a lie and get away with it until the day I die. But then comes our judgment with he on a throne in heaven on high, who knows all by his all-seeing eyes, then it would be me with tears in my eyes, when I had to see how I hurt you with my little white lies.

To really get the most out of life, we need to nurture relationships with those in our life. It is easy to find fault in anyone. But if you look for the good qualities and compliment on them, you may be pleasantly surprised that you will see more of them.

I think blessings are like a soft, gentle rain falling down from the sky. They fall lightly upon us and all around us every day. Too often, people are so busy waiting to witness a miracle in tsunami proportions that they are blind to gentle, constant falling rain of daily blessings.

Angel wings

Life without God is like an unsharpened pencil—it has no point!

—Unknown

No man ever steps in the same river twice, for it is not the same river and he's not the same man.

—Heraclitus

Jesus paid a debt he didn't owe, because we owed a debt we couldn't pay.

—Unknown

AFTERWORD

Public speaking in Leitchfield, Kentucky (August 8, 2012)

After being severely wounded during the war in Iraq in 2006, I began a new journey on what would be a very long road to recovery. The war ended for me and another began; my war after the war was learning to survive in a world with the severe handicaps I have. This war I will fight for the rest of my life.

I had major craniofacial reconstructive surgeries. I broke the sixth vertebra in my neck, which healed wrong, causing some right-side stenosis (restricted blood flow to my brain), which is probably the cause of my left-side neglect (my brain does not often recognize the world on my left side).

I am legally blind. I had my right eye removed, while I do not have any bilateral fields of vision in my left eye, and only see an area about the size of a paper plate at any one time. I still have a small amount of useable vision in my left eye (for which I am very thankful).

I realize a totally blind person would give anything to be able to have the sight I have.

I am legally deaf, although I can hear a limited amount via a hearing aid in my right ear. I have received a cochlear implant in my inner left ear, and I am hopeful and optimistic that one day I may be able to hear some sounds from the stereo again.

Although I am legally deaf, I still have some ability to hear. I realize a totally deaf person would give anything to be able to have the limited ability to hear that I have.

I have an abnormal gait. I require the use of a blind-man cane and a support cane to get around. Sometimes I need a walker, a wheelchair, or an assistant to get around. But for the most part, I can get around with the use of an aid of some kind on my own feet.

I realize that someone who is totally restricted to a wheelchair or who is paralyzed would give anything to have my mobility problems.

While I have been on a liquid or soft diet for the better part of five years, I realize that someone with a feeding tube would give anything to be able to be on my diet.

I have some memory problems. I suffer from severe post-traumatic stress disorder (PTSD). Someone with Alzheimer's disease would give anything to be able to remember things—even nightmares or traumatic events I imagine.

I guess all I am trying to point out is that no matter how bad things are for each of us, no matter what our trials or how heavy the burdens that we shoulder, there is always someone who has it worse than we do and would joyfully swap their troubles for ours.

I know this does not make our burdens lighter. It does not make pain hurt less. It does not make financial worries disappear. What I believe it can do, however, or how I use this knowledge, is from perspective. By reminding myself it could be worse, I find strength to endure while I put up a fight.

By changing my perspective of how I look at my problems, I have found that I have also been able to find new ways to deal with them—positive ways. I have found that just being able to have a more positive outlook on my situation can indeed make me feel better and often see a different way of doing things that can make the way I deal with my handicaps and burdens a lot easier.

Thinking of just one positive thought, or one thing to be grateful for each day, and reminding myself of that one thing throughout the day when things start to feel overwhelming to me often help to hold off a bout with the depression monster that usually stops by my place every day, wanting to come inside and play.

My Gordy-isms are that one thought each day for me. It is just another tool for my toolbox, along with many others, to help me get through each day.

I do believe a positive attitude, smiles, and laughter have a healing power. They certainly are not a cure-all, but they sure help.

I hope you found some of my Gordy-isms did just that: made you smile, laugh, and for a moment, no matter how brief, took your mind off your own troubles or worries.

Better still, I hope that perhaps they have inspired you to think of your own positive "isms" each day to ponder on and find joy in.

I hope then, that perhaps one day, you will share your positive thoughts, your own "isms," with me.

An optimist will always see the glass filled halfway as being half-full rather than half-empty!

By the way, do you know how an engineer will always view the half-full glass? They view it as a container that is twice as big as it needs to be for the volume of liquid it is holding (ha-ha).

When in doubt, smile.

Add me as a friend on Facebook to read the Gordy-isms I continue to post regularly: Gordon Ewell from Eagle Mountain, Utah.

http://www.facebook.com/gordy0406

You can also find me in

www.dunginmyfoxhole.com

www.alifetimeatwar.com

www.blustarriders.com

I can also be contacted by e-mail at
gordyewell@yahoo.com

Nothing is worth more than this day.—Goethe

My name may not be in the neon lights yet, but it has found its way to a couple of billboards. Got to start somewhere, I suppose; and it can't always be at the top.

2012

ABOUT THE AUTHOR

Master Sergeant (MSG) Gordon L. Ewell was born on June 8, 1967, and graduated from Emery County High School in May 1985. He joined the Utah Army National Guard on August 28, 1985, with initial assignment to the 1457th Engineer Battalion as a combat engineer. In August 1991, he transitioned to the Active Guard Reserve program, with Delta Company, of the 1457th Engineer Battalion.

His twenty-four-year career has been marked with distinction through notable accomplishments that render him an excellent example for other soldiers to follow.

Throughout his outstanding military career, he has served in key positions as training and administration specialist, supply sergeant, combat engineer squad leader, and personnel section sergeant.

From MSG Gordon L. Ewell's initial entry into military service, his superiors recognized his outstanding initiative and a deep care for his fellow soldiers. He has been recognized as one who would do whatever it takes to accomplish the mission or help a fellow soldier in need. His twenty-four-year career has been marked with distinction through notable accomplishments. Master Sergeant Ewell has graduated from over thirty army resident schools, graduating as the honor graduate, or in the top 10 percent of his class, from nearly every one of them.

He has completed, with a superior rating, over one thousand hours of army correspondence training. Additionally, he earned an associate of science degree in April 1999.

During his service in Iraq, Master Sergeant Ewell performed fifty-nine challenging and dangerous missions, which involved both the coordination of convoy route clearance and route clearance observation missions, based upon his knowledge and expertise in these areas. Master Sergeant Ewell was vital in the creation of the first route clearance handbook and was further recognized by the corps staff as the multinational corps subject matter expert in route clearance. His lessons learned in Iraq have been published in many army periodicals.

Master Sergeant Ewell led over 33 percent of the missions he was on in Iraq. He was recognized by his superiors to be unparalleled in his physical stamina and toughness complemented with superior technical and tactical capabilities. This was clearly demonstrated on the battlefield when his efforts under heavy enemy fire were unrivaled, which earned him a Bronze Star Medal, the Purple Heart Medal, and the Combat Action Badge.

During his combat missions, on six separate occasions, a vehicle he was in was blown up by improvised explosive devices (IEDs). One of the explosions was so powerful that it blew impacted wisdom teeth out the side of his jaw. In addition to major jaw damage, he suffers from broken vertebrae in his neck, damage to his lower spine, and permanent loss of hearing (leaving him legally deaf).

He suffered the anatomical loss of his right eye and peripheral and bilateral vision loss in his left eye, leaving him legally blind. He has a traumatic brain injury (TBI), flaccid neurologic bladder, loss of balance, an abnormal gait, and is fighting to overcome post-traumatic stress disorder (PTSD).

Master Sergeant Ewell returned from combat duty in December 2006 and was assigned to the 640th Regiment (Regional Training Institute). Because of the severity of his combat injuries, he was medically retired from injuries sustained while at war, in February 2010.

His medical journey to date has included six major surgeries, treatments in eight different hospitals, in three different states, by over forty-seven different doctors, surgeons, specialists, and other health care professionals, not counting the more than a dozen different dentists, endodontists, oral surgeons, and other dental specialists.

Today, though he is 100 percent disabled, he continues to serve with distinction, as a member of the Blue Star Riders, as a volunteer at the George E. Wahlen VA Hospital in Salt Lake City, with the Veterans of Foreign Wars, the Disabled American Veterans, and the American Legion.

The retired master sergeant currently resides in Eagle Mountain, Utah. He enjoys being a father and watching his babies grow.

He also enjoys public speaking, writing, helping other veterans, and the beach.

Military Awards and Decorations

Bronze Star Medal
Purple Heart Medal
Meritorious Service Medal
Army Commendation Medal (with bronze oak leaf)
Army Achievement Medal
Army Good Conduct Medal (with six bronze knots)
Army Reserve Components Achievement Medal (with three bronze oak leaves)
National Defense Service Medal (with bronze star)
Iraq Campaign Medal (with campaign star)
Global War on Terrorism Service Medal
Armed Forces Reserve Medal (with "M" device and silver hourglass)
NCO Professional Development Ribbon (third award)
Army Service Ribbon
Overseas Service Ribbon
Army Reserve Components Overseas Training Ribbon (third award)
Combat Action Badge
Diver and Mechanic Badge (with wheeled vehicle clasp)
Sharpshooter Weapon Marksmanship Badge
Utah Commendation Medal (third award)
Utah 2002 Olympic Winter Games Service Ribbon
Utah Emergency Service Ribbon
Utah Achievement Ribbon
Utah Recruiting Ribbon
Utah Service Ribbon
Joint Meritorious Unit Award
Army Superior Unit Award

Noteworthy Civilian Achievements

Presented the key to the city of Leitchfield, Kentucky, by Honorable Mayor William H. Thomason on August 12, 2012

Commissioned as a Kentucky colonel by the Honorable Governor Steven L. Beshear and the Honorable Secretary of State Alison Lundergan Grimes, of the Commonwealth of Kentucky, August 10, 2012 (the 221st year of the commonwealth)

Made an honorable duke of the city of Paducha, Kentucky, by Honorable Mayor Hardy Gentry on August 10, 2012

Was honored to be made an honorary member of Rotary International, with membership in the Park City, Utah Sunrise Club (August 15, 2011)

Elected as the senior vice commander of his Disabled American Veterans section, Wasatch One, Utah. (August 3, 2011)

Selected as vice president of the Blue Star Riders, honoring and helping our nations hospitalized soldiers and their families (September 2010)

Was one of six people from Utah selected to hand-stitch the Utah section onto the National 9/11 Flag, which now resides at the museum at Ground Zero as a national memorial and treasure (July 2011)

Received the State of Utah Department of Public Safety Executive Award of Merit in recognition and appreciation of extraordinary service and outstanding contributions on behalf of the citizens of Utah (2008)

Presented City of Eagle Mountain Outstanding Citizenship Award (2007)

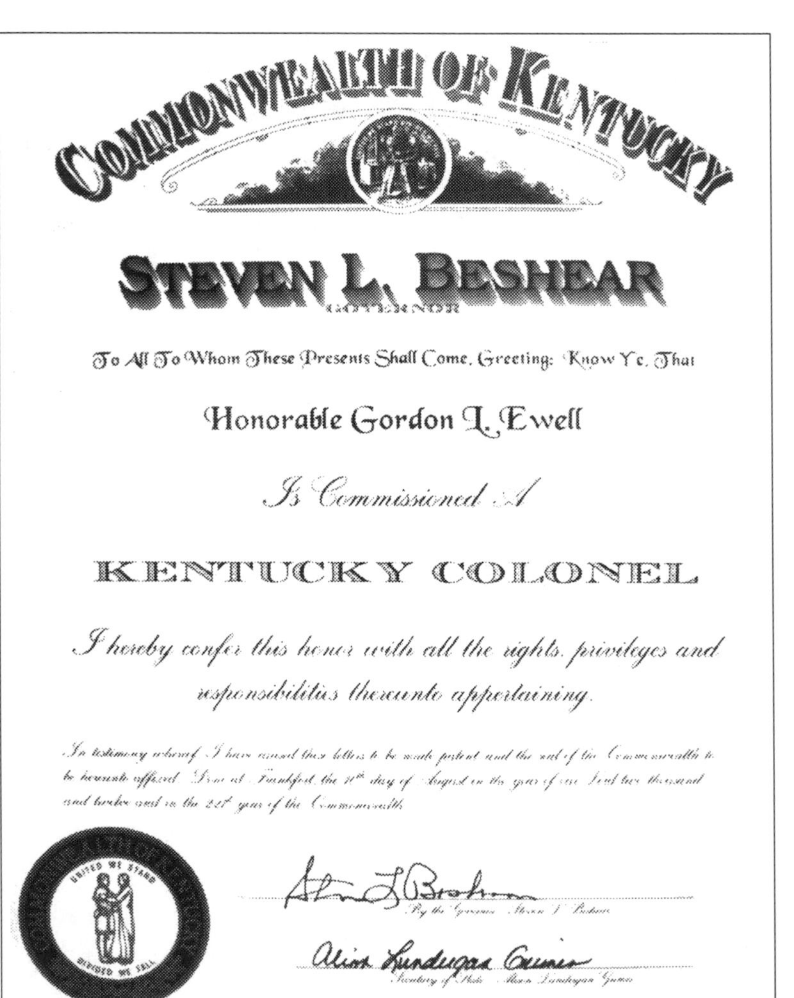

COMMONWEALTH OF KENTUCKY

STEVEN L. BESHEAR

GOVERNOR

To All To Whom These Presents Shall Come, Greeting: Know Ye, That

Honorable Gordon L. Ewell

Is Commissioned A

KENTUCKY COLONEL

I hereby confer this honor with all the rights, privileges and responsibilities thereunto appertaining.

I was presented with the highest honor awarded by the Commonwealth of Kentucky, a Kentucky colonel, by the Kentucky secretary of state, the Honorable Alison Lundergan Grimes.

My Kentucky family (*left to right*): John Barton, Carole Duke, Anthony Noe, me, Dr. Peter Trzop, and my brother Jim Lish and his wife, April; great people and volunteers.

Being presented with a certificate of achievement and the key to the city of Leitchfield, Kentucky, by the Honorable Mayor William H. Thomason.

Leading the assembly in the Pledge of Allegiance at a town hall meeting with the Honorable Congressman Jason Chaffetz (Utah); my dear friend Dell Smith (*center*), in Saratoga Springs, Utah.

The Honorable Governor of the State of Utah, Gary Herbert (*left*). A gentleman I am proud to call friend.

With Utah assistant to the secretary of the army, Mr. John Edwards; my friend and friend to all veterans, military service members, and their families.

U.S. ARMY

ACKNOWLEDGMENTS

I was, in a nutshell, a bomb hunter during the war in Iraq in 2006, at a time when incidents with improvised explosive devices (IEDs), or roadside bombs, were peaking at over three thousand one hundred a month, over one hundred a day, every day! An incident being either a bomb we found or one that found us. I was in a vehicle that was blown up, literally six different times, by a roadside bomb within ten feet of the vehicle and a seventh time by a mortar round that landed next to the vehicle I was in. In essence, I feel I cheated death seven times. It is a very small family, those with the mission of route clearance. I lost several "brothers" I had forged good friendships with, "brothers" who by one single bomb made themselves a memory to me. It was hard then. It remains so today. I was very severely wounded. I suffered a very long and painful recovery and am still suffering. However, I am alive. My friends are not. I count each day as a blessing. That being said, I feel everyone in my life is a blessing—literally! I feel like I need to acknowledge everyone who has made an impact on my life and everyone who is in my life today! Let me rephrase that. Because I do feel so blessed by everyone in my life, I *want* to list by name and acknowledge *everyone* who is in my life. There is truly *none* of you whom I am not thankful for in my life or whom I do not feel has been the inspiration for a positive thought or Gordy-ism that has helped me along my recovery road. To do so, however, would take more pages than there are in this book. The thought of this alone makes me feel very humbled and feel very blessed. For this warmth in my heart, I thank you all.

I want to acknowledge my Facebook friends who have given me feedback about my Gordy-isms, as I have posted them regularly, and encouraged me to keep doing so.

I am especially thankful for some old friends that have resurfaced, found me, and been a big source of strength to me, proving to me as well that true friendships never die, friends like Adam Gunn, Stacy Skinner, Randy Jones, Bob Grant, Maile Stackpole, Kelly Killpack, Clay Gremel, Elvin Anderson, Darin Grange, Sheri Vetere, Shawn McCourt, Barbie Potter, David Northrup, Roberta Poglajen, Linette Deason, Dana Jensen, Michale Willardson, Cheryll Tsushima, Trudi Cox, Rick Rowley, Cindy Funk, and Michael Mower.

Thanks to my family in the bluegrass of Kentucky: Jim and April Lish, Lois Hall, Dick Heaton, Misty Embry Thomas, Dr. Pete Trzop, John Barton, Joan Deyo, Anthony Noe, Carol Duke, Robert Bryant, Larry Crabbtree, Scott Dalton, Mayor Hardy Gentry, Mayor William Thomason, and Ron Stiers.

Thank you to Stacy Bare and PW Covington for being on the tip of the spear, fighting the good fight for veterans.

Thank you to Lucy and Leah for your inspiration.

Thank you to all my friends in Oscoda, Michigan.

Thank you to Dana and *all* my AmpSurf friends and family: Vicki Richardson, Annette Reder, Ed Ingles, and Courtney Wilson (thanks for staying in touch). Thank you to all my friends, employees, and volunteers, at the veterans hospitals in Salt Lake City, Utah, and Palo Alto, California. I appreciate all you have done to help, rebuild, support, and encourage me.

Thank you to my Homes for Our Troops family, especially to John Gonsalvez, Dawn Teixiera, Tom Benoit, Maura McGowan Yanosick, and Marissa Santos.

Thank you to Brandi and little "Sophers" for keeping me grounded.

Thank you to Vickey Lopes (and Tony) for staying so close, to Nola Pedersen Mikich for your kind heart, and Marie Nuccitell for constant encouragement.

Thank you to my friend Montel Williams for his example of never giving in when battling long-term illness or disability and for all you have done for me.

Thank you to Ann Jensen for a family friendship that reflects unconditional love (and for her special Christmas bush).

I can't say enough about my Aunt Marilynn; I love you dearly (Merrell and Alan too).

Thank you to a special friend at war in Afghanistan.

Thank you for believing in pixie dust

Thank you to Jeff Sagers whose friendship is solid as a rock!

To my dear friends Dell and Connie Smith, who have ensured I have been able to participate in functions and activities that are important to me and for always being there for me, I am so very grateful and humbled to be your friend.

Richard Hamilton, I love you tons. A man could not find someone who would never stop giving from his heart and caring for you, for another person or creature on the planet than you, Wolf. I am honored to be your friend (Marsha too)!

Jack Nitz, my friend, you are a giant among men!

Mom and Dad, I love you! You have shown, literally, that no matter the time, day or night, no matter the trouble or circumstance, no matter the cost, financially or of your time, your energy, or your hearts, that you will always be there for me—true unconditional love!

I could not have brothers or sisters who are loved more than I love mine. They are all examples and sources of strength to me.

To my little princesses, Scarlett Olivia and Lincoln Abbygale, Daddy loves you more than you could ever know. You were too small when Daddy got hurt to know much about or have a memory of how badly daddy got hurt. You are the reasons Daddy never gave up and never stopped fighting to get better, the reasons Daddy will always keep fighting so that I will always be able to love and care for you, and play with, protect, and provide for you also. You are what are most special in the treasure chest of my heart, the brightest stars in my night sky! I love you to the moon and back!

With my princesses Scarlett and Lincoln, September 2012

Reflections
Scarlett (*above*) and Lincoln (*below*), September 2012

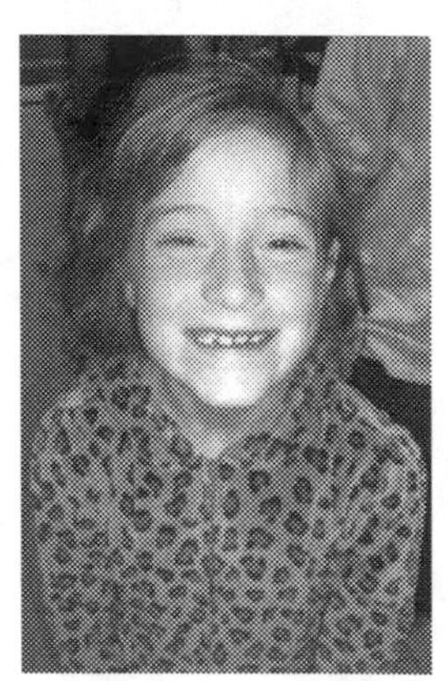

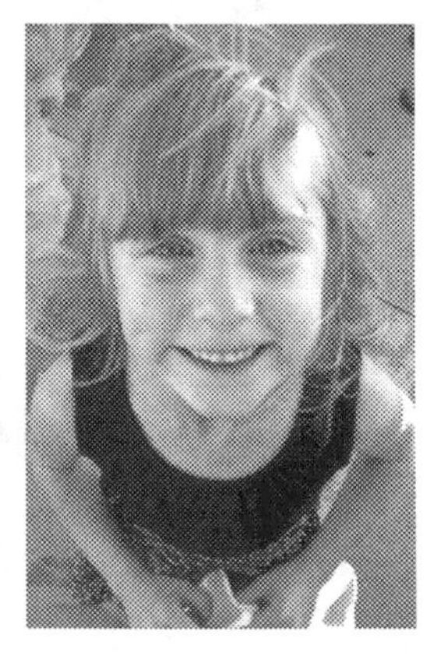

My princesses Scarlett and Lincoln (summer of 2012)

With my brother Wade at a Montgomery
Gentry concert, July 8, 2012

My dear friend and brother John Glines, August 2012

Above: with awesome K105FM radio talk show host Misty Thomas, of the live radio show *In the Know*

Below: with Jim Lish on the live call-in show that aired on August 10, 2012, in Leitchfield, Kentucky

Above: with WHAS channel 11 Kentucky TV news reporter Brooke Katz (interviewed on August 14, 2012)

Below: ABC channel 4 Utah morning show *Good Things Utah* cohost Nicea Degering (on show September 12, 2012)

Doing a live TV interview on the ABC channel 4 Utah morning show *Good Things Utah,* from the Healing Field in Sandy, Utah, on September 11, 2012

Below: (*left to right*) "Gordy" Ewell, Lt. Colonel Brock McLean (Ret.), *Good Things Utah* cohost, Brianne Johnson, and Show Anchor, Ann Sterling

Left: Sawn Swenson from Colonial Flag at the Healing Field in Sandy, Utah (September 11, 2012)

Right: with Jim Lish at the Hope Rising memorial in Sandy, Utah, (September 11, 2012)

My first surfing experience thanks to AmpSurf!

Above: AmpSurf instructor and friend Annette Reder

Below: My instructor, mentor, and friend Brad Howe

at the Wine Waves and Beyond Celebration in
Pismo Beach, California (June 3, 2012)

My first kayaking experience!

Thanks to Team River Runner, Salt Lake City, Utah.

Above: with Martine and Tim Troy, my instructors

Below: Tim pushes me into the water for the first time

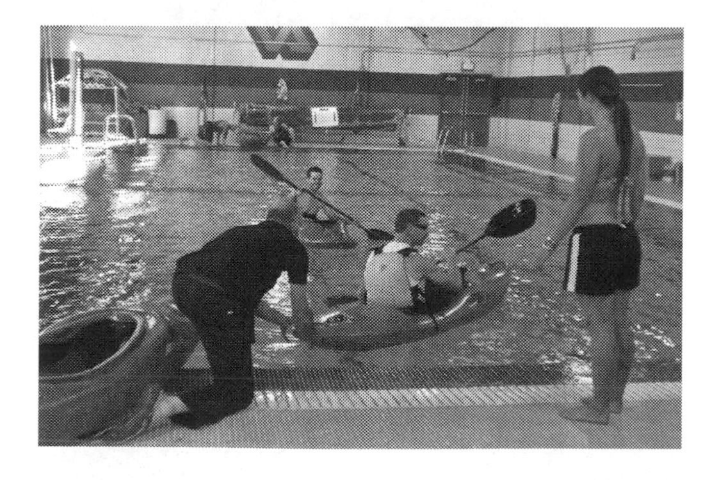

At La Jollie Beach in San Diego, California
(September 19, 2012)

Above: Catching a nice wave

Below: With actress and model Bo Derek

Doing a book signing in Bardstown, Kentucky, with Kentucky State American Legion sergeant at arms, Jim Lish

In memory of my dear friend

Dennis Cattell

Airborne, special forces, ranger,
Vietnam veteran gentleman, and friend to all

July 28, 1948-September 1, 2011

All gave some . . .

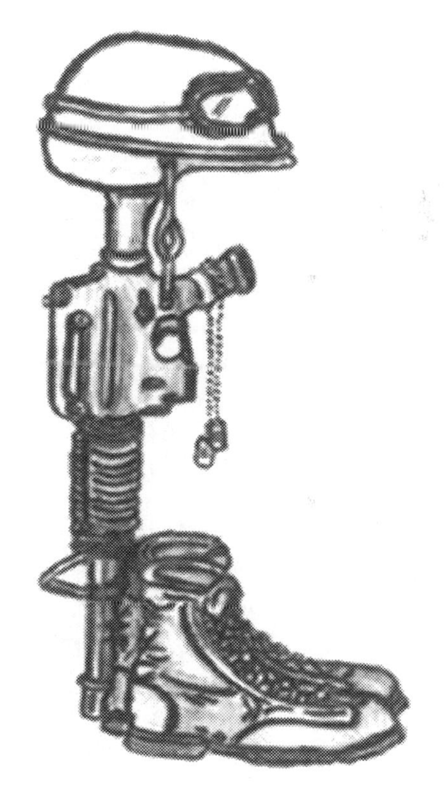

some gave all!

Some are still giving!

THE END